MW01643904

THROUGH THE EYE — OF THE — NEEDLE

Can I get to heaven if I have money?

DAN HAMLET

Dan Hamlet
info@EyeoftheNeedleBook.com
www.EyeofftheNeedleBook.com

Through the Eye of the Needle, Dan Hamlet —1st ed.

CONTENTS

PREFACE

My wife and I just had a friend over for coffee. This friend at one point owned a coffee shop and is a passionate barista. He offered some advice on how to get more out of our little home espresso machine and make better coffee. My reaction was, "Great! I get to learn from someone who is way smarter than me about coffee!" My wife's reaction was, "I'm sorry my coffee is not up to your standards. It's probably not worth making coffee for you again. I'll find something else to share with you." Both are very human reactions, and neither is wrong.

Writing a book like this can be like being a trained barista offering advice to people who already love coffee and have been making good coffee for decades. As a reader, you may read this and say, "I knew 80% of this, but the 20% was a new way of looking at my discipleship. I appreciate the advice." Or you may read this and say, "I already know most of this; what I know is good enough, and my time is better spent serving the Kingdom in other ways."

If you are reading this book, your feet are probably already on the path of discipleship. I am writing this book in the spirit of the barista. I am excited about your journey and I have a few tips and ideas I have picked up along the way that I love sharing with fellow travelers. I hope and pray that you are reading this book because you are hoping to learn something that could help you in an area of your discipleship that you want to improve a little bit.

This book is not a formula or a set of financial tips. It is a call to discipleship, an invitation to trust the Master who leads camels through narrow gates, and a roadmap grounded in Scripture, prayer, and practical wisdom for living as a faithful steward in a world overflowing with treasures that can so easily distract us from the Treasure.

If you have ever asked, *"Lord, what would You have me do with what You have given me?"*-this book is for you.

If you have any tips to share back, I would love to hear them! Maybe the Holy Spirit will encourage me to write another book, and your ideas can help more people!

PART I

The Problem with Wealth

CHAPTER 1

Framing the Problem

His master said to him, 'Well done, good and faithful servant; you have been faithful over a little, I will set you over much. Enter into the joy of your Master.
— Matthew 25:21

No one can serve two masters, for either he will hate the one and love the other, or he will be devoted to the one and despise the other. You cannot serve God and mammon.
— Matthew 6:24

It is easier for a camel to go through the eye of a needle than for a rich man to enter the kingdom of God.
— Matthew 19:24; Mark 10:25; Luke 18:25

Look up ↑

The three Scripture passages above frame a spiritual tension for anyone who has achieved some level of success in life. On one hand, we are clearly called to be fruitful-to take the gifts we've been given and multiply them. On the other, we're warned again and again in Scripture about the dangers of wealth.

The Bible contains more than 200 explicit warnings about the love of money, greed, and the misuse of wealth. That's the bad news.

The good news? Over 2,500 verses that speak to how we are to live with wealth and possessions in a way that honors God.

And the better news? I don't intend to quote them all.

In these pages, I want to offer both a broad vision and some specific, practical suggestions for how devoted Christians can have and use wealth in a way that leads to hearing the most beautiful words ever spoken:

Well done, good and faithful servant. Enter into the joy of your Lord.

A New Kind of Problem

Before we solve a problem, we need to understand it clearly. So, let's begin there.

For most of human history, poverty wasn't a crisis-it was a constant. A tiny fraction of the population had wealth. The middle class? It barely existed. The vast majority of people lived in what we would now call extreme poverty.

But that is changing-dramatically.

A report from the nonprofit *Our World in Data* titled "The Short History of Global Living Conditions and Why it Matters" outlines how the world began to shift 200 years ago. For millennia, roughly 80% of the global population lived in what today we call "extreme poverty." But as of 2018, that number had fallen to less than 10%.

The global middle class has grown from nearly nonexistent to around 15% of the world's population *even while the total population has increased sevenfold*. And the rate of wealth creation continues to accelerate. These categories are defined by the UN, and the data sets used for these numbers are based on census data from countries around the world.

I've seen this transformation firsthand. I grew up in South and Central America, and when I return today, the change is remarkable. Neighborhoods that once had tin roofs and no plumbing now have paved streets, running water, and cars in the driveway. The world is being lifted and it's happening fast.

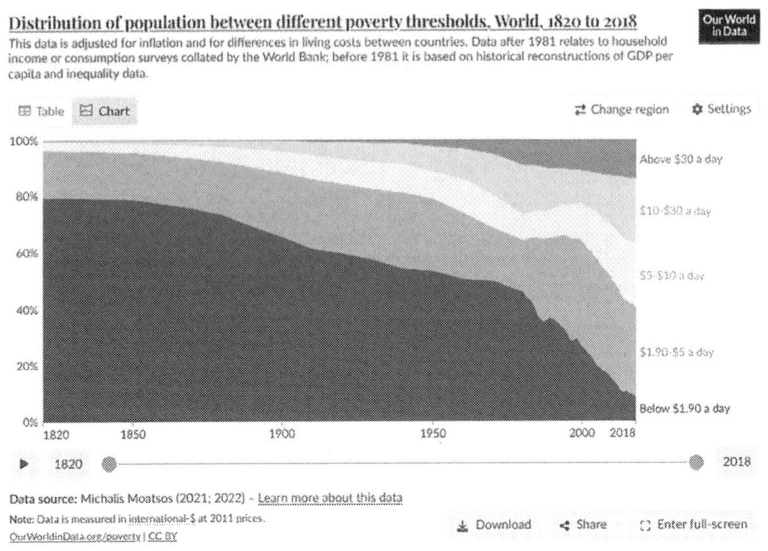

But With New Blessings Come New Questions

Eliminating poverty in our lifetime is thrilling for Christians. It's the kind of transformation we've prayed and worked for. But with this good news comes a new challenge — maybe even a more dangerous one.

What Do We Do with All This Wealth?

Jesus said it's harder for a rich man to enter the Kingdom of Heaven than for a camel to pass through the eye of a needle. If wealth makes it harder to get into Heaven, is it truly a good thing? That's the big picture question.

But here's the more personal one: *How can I lead myself and my family to Heaven if we have wealth?*

A Changed Landscape of Service

Let's look at this from another angle.

We are called to serve the poor. Jesus says in Matthew 25:40, "*Whatever you did for the least of these... you did for Me.*" It's a beautiful and direct call to emulate Christ by serving the vulnerable.

That used to be simple. When less than 1% of the population was middle class or better, there were plenty of people in need all around. You didn't have to look far.

But what about today?

If you live in a fully industrialized nation, truly poor people are harder to find. You might pass a few tents under an overpass on your commute, but you also pass thousands of cars. In many neighborhoods, there's not a poor person in sight.

So, how do we serve the poor in a world where poverty is increasingly rare, at least in our immediate surroundings?

Imagine this: every homeless shelter in America getting mobbed by middle-class Christians, all hoping to find someone to serve.

It's a ridiculous image but it illustrates something profound. We're entering a world where extreme poverty might become the exception, not the rule. And that means we need to rethink what it means to be faithful stewards in an age of abundance.

So Here's the Real Question

Wealth isn't going away. In fact, more of us will have more of it. The question for Christians today is not just, *What do I do with my money?*

It's deeper than that.

It's this: *How can I be the kind of person who has wealth—and not be owned by it?*

Let's begin answering that question together.

CHAPTER 2

The World's View of Wealth

Take care, and be on your guard against all covetousness, for one's life does not consist in the abundance of his possessions.
— Luke 12:15

The world's way of viewing possessions and wealth is fairly straightforward. If you study hard, work diligently, and manage your finances well, you can earn money. If you're careful with that money, you can build wealth and security — and, ultimately, buy things that make life comfortable for you and your family. When you die, whatever you haven't used can go to your children. We learned this worldview from our parents, our schools, and our society. It makes logical sense. It works.

But something is missing. Every Christian knows what it is if they take a moment to think about it. Yet, few of us have fully explored the implications of this missing element in our daily decisions and lives.

> *The world is God's, and everything in it.*
> — Psalm 24:1

We've heard this phrase and we know what it means when we pause to reflect, but most of us haven't fully applied this simple, powerful truth to money, work, and possessions.

A Closer Look at the World's View of Wealth

Let's examine what the world's view of money really means. According to this perspective, a great manager of money can grow in wealth, comfort, power, and influence. But does that make them happy?

I spent time in the mountains of Guatemala during my college years, and my wife and I went on a mission trip to Duran, Ecuador around the same time. In both places, we were struck by the happiness of the poorest people we had ever met. My parents used to visit the mountains of Morelia, Mexico for their anniversary mission trips, and they often took us along when we were young. They, too, remarked on the joy of the people we were there to "serve."

I'm sure many of you have had similar experiences.

In the world's view of wealth and possessions, the logical response to these encounters would be, "They don't know what they're missing," or perhaps simply, "How could they know how much better off we are?" After all, we had more wealth, security, power and influence.

We had air conditioning, more food than we could eat, books, computers, toys, cars, vacations, mission trips…

But they had joy - **real joy.**

Let me say that again.

They had joy-**and it was more abundant than ours.**

We had more wealth, but they had more joy.

Two Possible Conclusions

At this point, we can conclude one of two things:

1. They were backward, ignorant people who didn't know what they were missing.
2. We are missing something about joy.

As Christians, we know the answer.

Many books have been written about how our true joy comes from resting in the loving arms of our Creator. Joy and contentment are byproducts of loving and obeying God. This book is not one of those, so I won't delve too deeply into that topic here. But I'll get straight to the point: *Money does not bring joy or contentment.*

This is the critical flaw in the world's view of wealth.

The Illusion of Wealth's Power

The truth is, wealth doesn't bring joy. And for those who think it might, the sobering reality is that a remarkable number of millionaires-people who seemingly have it all- fall into despair. Many of them end their own lives despite their outward success.

> *I have learned the secret of being content in any and every situation, whether well - fed or hungry, whether living in plenty or in want. I can do all things through Christ who strengthens me.*
>
> — Philippians 4:11 - 13

Paul talks about his relationship with money in his letter to the Philippians. It is a tool and a gift from God. The problem isn't the wealth itself; it's the false belief that it can provide joy and contentment.

Does Holiness Mean Poverty?

So, if wealth doesn't bring joy, does that mean we need to become poor in order to experience true contentment?

That's certainly one approach. Church history is full of examples of individuals who gave up all their wealth, choosing radical poverty and holiness. If you feel that the Holy Spirit is calling you to this lifestyle, don't ignore that call.

In fact, look up the term "reverse tithe." You will encounter stories of modern, living examples of remarkable people who are living out that call to radical generosity. The Holy Spirit called them, and they answered the call.

But most of us aren't called to live in radical poverty. We have families to care for, businesses to run, clients to serve, and communities to lead. We've prayerfully answered the call to be right where we are, doing the work we're doing. So, how do we find or stay on *our* path to holiness?

How can we achieve true joy and contentment while still being stewards of wealth?

The Path to Holiness and Joy

We'll explore this path together. In the next chapters, we'll begin to unpack what it means to be faithful stewards of our resources and how we can walk in obedience while living in a world of abundance.

Stay with me as we take the next steps forward.

CHAPTER 3

Mammon

No one can serve two masters; for either he will hate the one and love the other, or he will be devoted to the one and despise the other. You cannot serve God and Mammon.
— Matthew 6:24

The word "mammon" comes from the Aramaic word *māmōnā* (ܡܡܘܢܐ), which means wealth or riches. In the New Testament, Jesus uses the term "mammon" in a negative sense, particularly in Matthew 6:24 and Luke 16:13, warning that you cannot serve both God and mammon. This admonishment implies that wealth can become an object of devotion, even idolatry when it is at the center of one's life.

I've been using the phrase "the world's view of money, wealth, and possessions." The word *mammon* neatly encompasses this idea, so for the remainder of this book, I'll try to use *mammon* to save some ink.

Let's take one more look at the difference between an ownership worldview and a stewardship worldview. Interestingly, this difference looks different depending on whether you are middle class, poor, or wealthy.

The Genius of the Poor, Middle Class, and Wealthy

Years ago, I volunteered as a mentor for high school students in South City St. Louis. Before meeting the kids, the mentorship program put us through training to help us understand that their worldview was different from ours. The program talked about the "genius" of the poor, the middle class, and the wealthy. This idea stuck with me because it helped me not only to have compassion but also to understand that what I thought I was saying might be heard completely differently by others.

What I'm about to share are broad generalizations or rough characterizations. They don't apply to every individual, of course. In fact, each person classified as "poor" or "wealthy" often varies significantly from these generalizations. Still, these distinctions were helpful in checking my assumptions and biases, helping me look at the person before me with fresh understanding.

The Genius of the Middle Class: Hope

The genius of the middle class is ***hope****.*

What this means is that, generally, middle- class individuals believe that if they sacrifice now, they can have something better in the future. They've seen their parents and grandparents do it.

They see their neighbors do it. It's how they buy houses, save for retirement, fund vacations, and invest in what matters to them. It doesn't always work perfectly, but it works enough that the exceptions are just that—exceptions.

The weakness of the middle class is ***comparison***.

Perhaps the most common question I get from a new middle-class client is some variant of the question: "How do I compare with others in my income level and age? Am I keeping up?" If a neighbor buys a new car, they start critically assessing their own vehicles. If their neighbor's kids are involved in certain activities, they start pushing their kids to do the same. It's difficult to be content when you're always comparing yourself to others.

The Genius of the Poor: Survival

The genius of the poor is ***survival.***

In general, the poor are experts at navigating through harsh conditions. They can survive in almost any environment — whether it's maneuvering through bureaucracies or relying on networks of charities. They expect the world to be a tough, unforgiving place, so they've learned to adapt, shift, and to go around obstacles.

The weakness of the poor is ***fatalism.***

The poor are often more content with what they have, but they have little faith that the world can improve for them. They know, from generations of evidence, that trying to save up or sacrifice for a better future is a fool's hope. They've learned to capture any windfall and use it immediately, because they *know* that the world is a hard place that will take from them. Saving for the future is frequently a wasted effort, because they are one car repair or other financial hardship away from having that savings stripped from them. Better to have that money buy them a tangible good now, than hope for a good in the future that likely won't materialize.

For example, many who've served the poor wonder why someone who struggles to pay their bills can still own nice things like multiple TVs, relatively new cars, etc. This may seem illogical to someone in the middle class. But for the poor, it makes perfect sense.

Having money, from a windfall or inheritance for example, can help the poor feel more secure against the hard world, but it can create a sense of paranoia because they are waiting for the world to take it from them. It is difficult for them to invest, or to save for future goods. The money often gets spent fairly quickly on homes, cars, vacations, etc. We know that lottery winners are often broke within five years, no matter how big the jackpot was. It is easy to judge that behavior, but it is internally consistent behavior based on generations of lived experience.

You can have middle-class or wealthy-class money but still have a poor mindset.

The Genius of the Wealthy: Responsibility

*The genius of the wealthy is **responsibility**.*

The wealthy don't need hope, they already have everything they need. If they want something they can get it. They have the means to influence their surroundings. They can shape their community with wealth, power, influence, and the respect they command.

*The weakness of the wealthy is **loneliness.***

The challenge for the wealthy is a fundamental distrust of others. They're often suspicious of people befriending them only because of their wealth, influence, or power. Their lived experience supports this distrust. As a result, the wealthy often interact only with other wealthy people-and do so cautiously. This distrust of the motives of possible friends creates an isolating, almost "gilded cage" effect, leaving many of them profoundly lonely.

The Curse of Mammon

All these worldviews place money at the center of their universe, and each of them carries the curse of mammon. Money can mean safety for the poor, but it also breeds paranoia. For the middle class, it can mean a leg up in life, but it also fuels constant comparison and a never-ending need to keep up. And for the rich, it can mean more power and influence, but it also brings isolation and crushing loneliness.

In all three cases people see money as the answer. From there it is a small step to make money our god.

No one can serve two masters; for either he will hate the one and love the other, or he will be devoted to the one and despise the other. You cannot serve God and Mammon.
— Matthew 6:24

All three world views place money at the center of their universe. All three carry with them the curse of mammon.

All three are traps.

CHAPTER 4

Eye of the Needle: Good Camel

"It is easier for a camel to go through the eye of a needle than for a rich man to enter the kingdom of God." When the disciples heard this, they were greatly astonished and asked, "Who then can be saved?" Jesus looked at them and said, "With man this is impossible, but with God all things are possible."
— Matthew 19:24–26

Jesus gave us a parable that was shocking in His time and remains shocking today. The camel parable came immediately after His conversation with the wealthy young man who, not content with having kept the Commandments, pressed Jesus for more-to ensure eternal life. Jesus told him to sell all he had, give to the poor, and follow Him. But the man walked away sorrowful, for he had many possessions.

This story of the young man and the camel parable that follows is familiar, and it's uncomfortable-especially for those of us who have achieved success in the world. Like that young man, many of us don't quite know what to make of it. Maybe that's why you picked up this book. Maybe this story has nagged at you for years, and you're hoping for some clarity. Well, let's give it a shot.

The History of the "Eye of the Needle"

The image of the camel and the needle's eye would've made immediate sense to Jesus' listeners. In ancient cities large gates in city walls were often built with a small pedestrian door in or next to them. These narrow doors-called "the eye of the needle"-allowed foot traffic while keeping the main gates securely closed.

Now, picture a camel. Tall, wide, and often laden with heavy packs of goods. That camel couldn't pass through the eye of the needle. It's a little absurd. Comical, even. But that image made the point vividly and humorously.

But here's the interesting part: a camel *could* make it through, just not by itself.

First, the camel had to be unloaded. All the goods, the burdens, the possessions-everything had to be removed by the master. Once unburdened, the camel was still too tall. So next, the camel had to kneel, often on a board. Only then, under the master's direction, could it be dragged through the gate.

Jesus told the young man to do two things: detach from his possessions and follow Him. He couldn't do it. None of us can—at least, not alone.

The camel didn't unload itself or kneel on its own. The master did that. *We* need the Master. *We* need to be guided, unloaded and carried into his Holy City.

Jesus finishes the moment with a powerful truth: "With man this is impossible, but with God, all things are possible." None of us—rich, middle class, or poor—can enter the Kingdom on our own. We all need the Master to carry us in.

As I mentioned in the previous chapter, the poor often find it easier to be content, simply because there's less to be attached to. Wealth makes detachment harder, which is exactly why this parable hit so hard back then, and still does today.

Whenever I feel like I'm drifting back into the mindset of ownership rather than stewardship, I come back to this parable of the camel.

In my prayer when I was asking for guidance for this book, this prayer came to me. Feel free to borrow it, adapt it, or make it your own:

A Prayer for the Good Camel

God, help me to be a good camel.

To recognize that everything I carry is Yours.

Some is Your gift to me from Your generous and loving heart.

Some I carry for others.

Help me to share with others, recognizing that it is not my love and generosity at work, but that it is Your love and generosity flowing through me.

And when it is time to pass through the narrow gate, help me to joyfully pass Your gifts to the next steward. As an obedient camel, help me to kneel humbly before You that You may carry me into Your Holy City.

Amen

PART II

Becoming a Steward!

CHAPTER 5

I Want to Be a Steward!

Commit your way to the Lord; trust in Him, and He will act.
— Psalm 37:5

Stewardship.

Some may cringe at that word. Many churches use it as code for "time to ask for money." I grew to dislike the term myself after serving on a stewardship committee at church-because that was always the context. Maybe you've had similar experiences.

But I want to redefine that word for you in this book.

Stewardship begins with what the mammon worldview is missing: "*The world is God's, and everything in it.*" Everything we have in this world—including the place and time where we were born, the families we were born into, and the skills, talents, and abilities we possess—is a gift from a loving God. The money we earn, the businesses we build, our marriages, our children,they are all gifts.

We own nothing.
We are stewards of His gifts while we are on this earth. The secret of joy and contentment begins here.

So now you're trying to believe this. You're leaning in. But what does it mean? How do you actually live it out? How is it different from what you already do when you pray?

Let's break it down.

Start With Vocation and Purpose

Your primary purpose on this earth is to love and serve the Lord. You've heard that before, from pastors, books, or Scripture itself. But there's more: God also has a specific plan for each of us.

That plan comes in two forms:

- A **general plan** we find in Scripture and the teachings of the Church.
- A **personal plan** that is revealed in prayer and in conversation with the Holy Spirit.

Your **vocation** is the first piece of that personal plan. Vocare is Latin meaning "to call." Your vocation is your call to marriage, singleness, or religious life. Each is a path to holiness. It's not something you choose so much as something you answer. God's plan for us is better than our plan for ourselves, so listening for His call and answering it can lead us the life He has planned for us.

His plan may not be straightforward. My father was married for decades. After my mother passed, he later entered religious life. It was an incredible second vocation. He didn't decide on it as much as he answered the call when it came.

Many of you are already living your vocation. You're married with children, or you're single and serving your community, nieces and nephews, business, or church. Stewardship includes seeing these not as roles you play, but as callings you fulfill.

Write It Down

There's something transformative about writing down your priorities and goals. If you've done this before, you already know. Various studies show that people who write down their goals with specific details are **33–42% more likely to achieve them**. Writing it down makes it real. It creates accountability.

So write down your goals. These can include family, business, friendships, adventure, charity, quiet time, sports, writing—any wholesome activity. For example:

- I am on the earth to love and serve God, and to join Him for eternity.
- I will faithfully live out my God-given vocation to (be a spouse, parent, single servant, etc.)
- I will lead or serve in my profession with excellence and integrity.
- I will be a loyal and life-giving friend.
- My body is a temple. I will pursue fitness and health.

- I will champion the rights of the unborn through time and giving.
- I will serve children in my community as needed by supporting the school.
- I will know God in the beauty of His creation through travel and new experiences.
- I will support my children by supporting them in their sports and activities.

Write your own list. Don't worry about formatting; use a spreadsheet, a journal, sticky notes, whatever works. Just get it out of your head and onto paper.

Then **rank your goals,** pray through them, bring them to God in prayer, and ask Him to reorder them. Adjust as needed.

That's your foundation. And believe it or not, that's the hardest part! It is easy to say, "Write down your goals." But some part of us knows that to do so is to commit, so we resist.

Now let's move to the next step.

Budget Your Time

Now that you've defined your priorities, ask; How are you spending your time? Does it reflect what you just wrote?

For years, I have said health is important to me. I am a father of 7 and I started fatherhood late, when I was almost 30. I want to keep up with my kids now and any future grandkids! So, I connected health to my **faith** (my body is a temple) and my **vocation** (engaged husband, present father, active grandfather).

Full disclosure: When my schedule gets crowded, gym time is still the first thing I cut. That said, if I hadn't written down health as a top priority and linked it to my deeper purpose, I'd probably never go.

I once walked a very successful client through this process of goal setting. He'd been writing down business goals for years, and his business was thriving. But when I asked if he'd ever done that for his personal life, he blinked.

The truth? His home life was unraveling. His marriage was distant. His relationships with his kids were shallow. His family finances were chaotic, even as his income soared. A year later, after applying the same disciplined process he used so well at work to his home and family life, everything had started to turn around: His marriage was healing, his time with his kids was improving, and they were finally living within their means.

The family was beginning to manage its finances, eliminate debt, and reign in the spending that had been compensating for a lack of warmth and intimacy. They were ready to start setting bigger goals and creating plans to achieve them.

So-where are **you** spending your time? How does your calendar line up with your priorities? If you are anything like me, or like most of my clients frankly, there is a serious disconnect between what we say is important, and how we budget our time.

The first time I asked myself that question, I realized I was giving maybe 10–15 minutes a day to prayer, including mealtime and bedtime with the kids. I was certainly not "tithing" with my time. I said that God was the most important thing in my life, but I spent very little time talking to Him.

If we're awake 16 hours a day, 10% of our time is **96 minutes**. My first reaction? "What would I even talk to God about for that long?" and "I don't even talk to my wife that much!"

And yet, I had no problem working 10+ hours a day.

Now I don't hit 96 minutes every day, but I've changed how I start my day. I read Scripture first thing. I reflect on it while working out. After dropping the kids at school, I spend at least 30 minutes with God in church before heading to the office. At noon my phone alarm goes off and I try to do a five - minute Examen – an exercise of reflection on the first part of the day, trying to improve my awareness of God's presence in every interaction. In the evening, family prayer time has stretched out and gotten more meaningful. And my wife and I now pray together before we go to sleep every evening.

When we get through it all (we do have 7 children with all the chaos that implies), this rhythm has **transformed our home, our marriage, my work, everything.** God is now at the center, and because of that, everything is more fruitful.

Tithing of time is not specifically a scriptural thing. It is a concept I used for myself to gauge my prayer life. Scripturally we are called to *"Rejoice always, pray without ceasing, give thanks in all circumstances" 1 Thessalonians 5:17*. It was a useful tool to help me bring prayer more intentionally into every part of my life. In prayer we are called to include God in every aspect of our lives, to be aware of His presence constantly around us and to move and act accordingly. I wasn't living like that, so the prayer "tithe" was a good tool to help me get moving in the direction of constant prayer that Paul calls us to.

What If Your Life Is Already Broken?

You might be reading this and thinking,"Too late." Maybe your marriage is over. Your kids are distant. Your health is in pieces. Your career is in shambles.

Here's the truth:

- **Yes**, our sins—and the sins of others—can do terrible damage to our lives
- **But**, God can redeem **any** situation and create beauty from ashes.

What can you do?

Start with where you are.
Write down your values.
Put God first.
Tithe your time to pray to your loving Creator.

Let God speak into your plan.

Then begin to budget your time according to the priorities that you and God have agreed on.

Your life will change.

Stewardship Starts Here

The first step to living a life of stewardship is to define what stewardship means for **you**. Write down your priorities. Rank them. Pray over them, asking God to shape your priorities according to HIS plan for you.

This is the hardest part. But once you've built this foundation, everything else in the coming chapters can fall into place.

CHAPTER 6

Money Follows Mission

But seek first the kingdom of God and His righteousness,
and all these things will be added to you.
— Matthew 6:33

Money Follows Mission

My dad often says, "Money follows mission." He's one of the smartest men I know, and I try to pay attention when he repeats himself. He's also been there at the beginning of more than one Holy Spirit-inspired mission over the last few decades. After my mom passed away, my father answered a call to go to the seminary and become a priest.

Back in the 1990s, he supported a little grassroots idea in his parish that turned into Mobile Loaves and Fishes in Austin, Texas founded by Alan Graham. It started with retrofitted food trucks—old "roach coaches"—filled not only with sandwiches, but also with socks, toothbrushes, and other basic necessities. Volunteers didn't just drop things off and drive away; they got out and sat with the homeless, listened to their stories and learned their names. Entire families volunteered and joined in truck teams. They learned that socks and toothbrushes, surprisingly, were among the most prized possessions on the street. The movement spread across the country, because it met a real human need and did so with dignity and love.

Today Mobile Loaves and Fishes has thousands of volunteers in several states. The have also pioneered an innovative resettlement program called Communities First that is helping the homeless move off the streets into their own home. The Holy Spirit blessed these initiatives.

Money follows mission.

More recently, my dad launched a scholarship program to help immigrant families in Austin, Texas send their children to Catholic schools. In a church of more than 2,500 families, he discovered that only 7 had children enrolled in religious education. He made an offer: Bring him an acceptance letter to a Catholic school and pay the first dollar — he'd find a way to cover the last dollar and ensure that child would be able to attend that school. The only "string" was that the parents had to bring their children to church regularly. There was no deep pool of money. No multi-year pledge campaign. Just obedience to the Holy Spirit and a belief that God would provide.

Today, this "Our Kids at Heart" scholarship fund pays over a million dollars in tuition every year, sending over 250 children to Catholic schools in four cities. These aren't just educational wins — they're family transformations. He calls the children his little "Pentecost bombs." When the kids come home full of Scripture and faith, singing Christian hymns they learned at school, their parents start coming back to church. The children are evangelizing their families. Troubled marriages are healed. The entire family gets involved in church life. They *all* become disciples.

Soon, church ministries filled up with volunteers. More ministries were born. The seven weekend Masses became standing-room only. And a parish that used to run in the red suddenly had every ministry funded and overflowing with volunteers.

The Holy Spirit blessed this initiative. Money follows mission.

Why This Matters to You

These stories are great, but what do they have to do with your personal stewardship?

Everything.

Because the same principle applies to us. When we align our time, talent, and treasure with the movement of the Holy Spirit, good flows from it. Sometimes big and visible, sometimes quiet and hidden, but always good. We've seen it happen in churches and nonprofits. It can happen in our families too.

Budgeting as a Steward

The world teaches us to budget by asking, "Do I have enough?" And when the answer becomes "yes," we move on to, "What else can I buy now?" The whole point of the worldly budget is to calculate how much we can spend. The answer is always "All of it. Every dollar."

But a steward asks a very different question: "How much is enough?"

That question is tethered to your purpose. It's rooted in your priorities-the ones you and your spouse (if applicable) prayerfully ranked in the last chapter. When you have funded everything on that list, you draw a line. That line is your **finish line**, the point where spending on yourself ends, and Kingdom giving begins.

If you ask, "Do I have enough," your list is infinite. There's always another want, another toy, another upgrade. You will never reach the end.

But when you ask "how much is enough," you're working from a finite list. You can finish it. And when you finish, the overflow has a mission.

To Do: Sit down (alone or with your spouse) and look at your current budget. Ask honestly: Are our Kingdom priorities showing up here? If money follows mission, are we living our mission?

The Tithe

Tithing is often misunderstood. It simply means "a tenth." In the Old Testament, it was about giving first fruits, the best portion of your harvest back to God. Not the leftovers.

Remember Cain & Abel? They both brought offerings. But Abel's was accepted, and Cain's wasn't. Why? Abel gave his first and best. Cain gave something, but not the best. The issue wasn't the amount, it was the heart. Abel grew more united to God. Cain grew bitter and separated from God.

Malachi chapter three picks up this theme. God says:

> *Bring the full tithe into the storehouse, that there may be food in My house. Test me in this," says the LORD Almighty, "and see if I will not throw open the floodgates of heaven and pour out so much blessing that there will not be room enough to store it.*
>
> — Malachi 3:10

Tithing isn't for God's benefit. He doesn't need our money. He makes very clear in several places that He does not need or desire our burnt offerings. What He wants is our hearts.

> *For I desire steadfast love and not sacrifice, the knowledge of God rather than burnt offerings.*
>
> — Hosea 6:6

Here's the secret: God is LOVE! His is a generous heart! To draw close to Him, we must learn generosity. We must love what He loves—His Church, His people—and we give accordingly.

Tithing has two purposes:

1. It shows that we love God's Church, flawed as it may be. (Of course it's flawed; *we* are in it!)
2. It breaks the power money has over us.

Returning the first 10% of each week's wages or each project's profit to God reminds us that it is all his in the first place. It is easy to *say* that everything belongs to God. The tithe is the first place where we embody that statement, where we actually live out that conviction by physically giving back the first and best part. And thus the power of ownership is broken and we can begin to think like stewards. We can begin to act like it really is all God's, and he is entrusting it to us while we are here. We can begin to be trustworthy to God because we are not claiming what is his as our own.

Old Testament vs. New Testament Tithe

As God was training His people, over hundreds of years and dozens of generations, He brought them out of polytheistic worship and perverse lifestyles, forming them into a chaste, monotheistic, and holy people. In that season, He carved the Law in stone.

Then Jesus came and perfected the Law, showing us that what God really wanted was our hearts.

So, what does that mean for the 10% tithe?

For many Western Christians, and many churches, it's been taken to mean that the tithe is no longer required, as long as we give *something*. But if the reasons for the tithe are still valid—if we still find ourselves attached to love of Mammon—then we should still take the tithe seriously.

Personally, I know I still need to give a minimum of 10%. Something shifts in my heart when I reach or exceed that threshold. Generosity flows more easily. My trust in God increases. Life just seems to work better, as if there's a grace flowing. I feel so good, so free, that I'm frequently drawn to give more than 10%.

When I tithe like that (10% or more) it is easier for me to think like a steward, not an owner. And that shift is profound; it's like putting on blue-tinted sunglasses when you've only ever worn gray ones. The world looks different. My relationship with God's gifts feels different. It's hard to describe, but it feels like a supernatural grace—not something I accomplished, but something I received.

I would love for more people to feel that grace. I challenge you: Try it.

Tithe vs Alms

The church and the Bible frequently discuss giving alms. The term alms, however, has not been used much in Western culture lately, so we have lost a sense of its meaning. The best definition I have heard of alms (and I wish I could remember the source of this quote) is "giving from our wants to someone else's needs at the prompting of the Holy Spirit." This practice is different from tithing, though we often conflate the two.

What's the difference?

Tithe is giving back to God through His church.

Giving Alms is being the hands of the Holy Spirit by giving directly to Kingdom needs in the world.

A client once described Almsgiving like this, "I have a vacation fund. My neighbor's house just burned down. The Spirit confirmed in prayer that my neighbor needs my vacation fund more than I need a vacation."

Almsgiving is spontaneous, Spirit–led and personal. Alms is the Good Samaritan.

It's the friends lowering the paraplegic through the roof to Jesus.

It's keeping granola bars in your car to hand out to the beggar under the highway.

It's bringing meals to the new parents or watching their kids while they go to a funeral or on a much-needed retreat.

It's adopting a child in a foreign country.

It's supporting the local pregnancy center or food pantry.

It's sending food and supplies to flood or hurricane devastated communities.

It's sitting with the person at the picnic that nobody wants to sit with.

Beyond Tithing & Alms-Structured Generosity

Once your needs are met and your **finish lines** drawn, you may find yourself with excess capacity. God has gifted you with everything you need for your family and responsibilities and has asked you to be steward over more! What is our responsibility when this happens?

The ownership mindset says, "Great! I can buy more." The stewardship mindset says, "Lord, who is this for?"

When we identify excess capacity as Stewards, we turn to the Owner and ask: "What is the purpose of this money?"

Frequently, we learn that we have been gifted with these extra resources to be stewards of them for someone else. One couple that I discussed this with revealed that their children were all either pastors or had married pastors, and they learned that it was their duty to provide for their children's retirement. So they structured their finances to fill that gap.

Another couple discovered in prayer that their business should grow to include more employees, so they could support another family. Their excess became investment capital to grow their business and hire someone.

When praying about these issues, some people determine that they are being called to invest in certain businesses, support certain causes or charities, or to set wealth aside for future philanthropy, which can take the form of direct donations, donor-advised funds, or family foundations. It can also change estate planning goals and tax strategies. Whatever the call, once they have some idea of what God is asking of them, we can start to plan and execute their calling carefully and responsibly, as good stewards.

This form of generosity is different from Tithing, which is a loving return to God of our first fruits through His Church. It is also different from Almsgiving which is the spontaneous giving from our wants to someone else's needs at the prompting of the Holy Spirit.

This third category of generosity is what I call **Structured Generosity**: careful stewardship of the wealth and resources that have been entrusted to us for the benefit of a Kingdom purpose, either now or in the future. Successful people who live financial lives bounded by their finish lines, living with a heart of stewardship, can now get excited when their business grows for reasons that are different than what the ownership worldview teaches.

In the ownership view, we get excited when our income rises because we can build more wealth and have nicer things. This excitement is fleeting and leaves us hungering for more. It does nothing to move us closer to eternal life with God.

A steward living within their finish lines, on the other hand, gets excited because he can do more for the Kingdom! That could be hiring and supporting more people, reaching more people with products and services that improve lives and serve human flourishing. It could be directly supporting organizations that do good works in our communities. It could be accumulating wealth in foundations or donor-advised funds aimed at supporting capital campaigns and larger, more expensive community efforts. The balance sheets of an owner and a steward could look similar, but the uses, outcomes and rewards are incredibly different.

Stewarding Debt and Assets–The Balance Sheet

Our cash flow on a day-to-day basis reveals where our heart truly lies. Good stewardship connects those cash flows to the priorities we've brought before God in prayer.

But stewardship doesn't stop with income and expenses, it shapes our balance sheet as well. So let's take a few minutes to talk about debt and assets.

> *The borrower is slave to the lender.*
> — Proverbs 22:7

Scripture offers consistent caution about the hazards of debt. It never calls debt sinful, but it clearly frames borrowing as unwise and lacking in prudence. So, what does that mean for us as stewards?

Owners often embrace debt because it allows them to enjoy something now and pay for it later. Unfortunately, this often leads to regret when they're still paying for something that no longer brings joy or has already been consumed.

Borrowing always mortgages our future in exchange for a present perceived good. That's not universally wrong. A home mortgage, for example, can provide a stable place to raise a family while children are still young enough to benefit from it.

But every debt carries a built-in temptation: to buy more than we need simply because "we can pay for it later." Temptation draws our hearts toward worldly goods, comfort and convenience, without asking God if now is the right time or if that good is even meant for us.

Debt can easily become a way of avoiding hard questions. It opens the door to relying on money—or future money—as a substitute for trusting in God's provision. When that happens, it begins to erode our dependence on Him and feeds a mindset that says, "I must provide for myself, no matter what."

If God truly owns everything, then using the money He hasn't yet given us to satisfy today's desires is a form of presumption. It puts our wants ahead of His timing. And while we may justify it in the moment, we often find ourselves burdened later, not just financially, but spiritually.

Some argue that borrowing shows a lack of trust that God will provide what we need. It's a nuanced conversation, one worth having over a meal with thoughtful friends. I believe there's some merit to it, though individual circumstances can be complex.

A home mortgage may be part of wise stewardship. Borrowing to expand a business might be a faithful use of resources. Emergency borrowing—like payday loans to feed a child or keep the heat on in winter—is heartbreaking and demands grace and discernment.

But in most cases, we're not borrowing strategically. We're borrowing to satisfy an immediate want, not in prayerful stewardship but in impatient ownership.

That's when debt becomes bondage; not just to the lender, but to our own desires. We're enslaved by the need to have now, rather than the discipline to wait or the faith to trust.

God can free us from that slavery. He invites us to trust Him more deeply and to be content with what He's already provided.

> *I have learned the secret of being content in any and every situation, whether well fed or hungry, whether living in plenty or in want. I can do all things through Christ who strengthens me.*
> — Philippians 4:11–13

Assets Present a Different Challenge...

If debt shackles us to our past decisions, assets tempt us to believe we've secured our future. But stewardship requires us to ask: *Are my assets serving God's priorities or mine?*

There's nothing inherently wrong with having wealth. Scripture includes faithful stewards like Abraham, Job, and Joseph, men of means. But in each case, their resources were put to work for God's purpose, not their personal comfort or ego. The question isn't how much you have, but whether your assets are aligned with your assignment.

A well-stewarded balance sheet doesn't just minimize liabilities; it actively mobilizes assets toward mission. Are your investments reinforcing your calling? Is your business supporting your community and family in redemptive ways? Does your home function as a sanctuary for hospitality and kingdom work - or just a monument to personal achievement?

A few years ago we consecrated our home to Christ. Our home is not ours. It is Christ's. We asked him "What is the purpose of this house? We got a clear sense that it was to be a place of hospitality to build community.

We try very hard to be the place where people drop their kids when there's an unexpected or weekday school closure, or the place where friends come when they need a cup and a conversation, or the backyard where friendships and memories are made.

When we sit and talk about what the house needs, we ask, "What do You want for Your home?" It's not our house, so we ask the Master this question regularly. This change in our relationship to the house we live in has led to some great conversations with our kids about what possessions are and what stewardship really means.

Remember: *Assets are tools, not trophies*. If they aren't serving your kingdom calling, they may be serving your ego instead. Don't just grow your net worth. Grow your eternal impact.

Examine Your Contingency and Protection Plan

If God called you home tomorrow, would your absence derail the people and causes you care most about? A core part of biblical stewardship is *preparing for the uncertainties of life in a fallen world*. That's where contingency planning comes in.

Many Christians shy away from this topic because it feels like planning for death or anticipating doom. But contingency isn't about fear, it's about faithfulness. It's about protecting the vulnerable and providing continuity for what God has entrusted to you.

This is where I encourage clients and friends to embrace the **3 P's of Love, not Fear**:

1. **Protect** your loved ones from financial harm. This protection may mean insurance, estate documents, or simply clearly communicated plans.

2. **Provide** a runway for them to continue the mission—whether that's education for your children, income for your spouse, or funding for a ministry.

3. But don't be **Paranoid**. You don't need to insure yourself against every possible future. That's not stewardship—that's fear masquerading as responsibility. Trust God's sovereignty even as you take wise steps.

Remember, we prepare not because we fear the future, but because we love the people God has entrusted to us.

Stewardship Means Defining the Finish Lines

One of the most powerful tools in a steward's arsenal is the concept of **finish lines**. These are predetermined limits—decisions made in prayer and wisdom—that keep us from drifting into ownership mode.

A finish line might look like:

- A cap on how much house is "enough."
- A limit on annual lifestyle spending, even as income grows.
- A target for savings or investments, beyond which excess is given away.

Finish lines *set us free*. They quiet the endless appetite for more. They allow us to enjoy what God has given without becoming enslaved to Mammon or cultural expectations.

They also keep us honest. Without them, it's easy to spiritualize lifestyle inflation or delay generosity until some vague, future season of "enough." With finish lines in place, we can joyfully declare, "This is sufficient. The rest is seed for the Kingdom."

A Steward's Balance Sheet Tells a Different Story

Owners accumulate to feel secure. Stewards allocate to stay obedient.

Owners build resumes. Stewards build altars.

Owners cling to assets. Stewards release them at God's prompting.

Take some time this week to look not just at your income and expenses, but your balance sheet. What is your life *really* saying about your priorities? About your trust? About your willingness to follow Christ not just with your words but with your wealth?

As Paul said, "*It is required of stewards that they be found faithful.*" (1 Corinthians 4:2)

Not successful.
Not admired.
Not independently wealthy.

Faithful.

PART III

Stewardship in Action

CHAPTER 7

Biblically Responsible Investing

Better is a little with righteousness than great revenues with injustice.
— Proverbs 16:8

"Did you consult the Bible before you bought into your investment portfolio?"

Robert Netzly asks this question in his book *Biblically Responsible Investing*. If you have the time, it's worth the read. Netzly's main point is simple but profound: the Bible does not skip over our investments. It offers us guidance not just for how to live our lives but also for how to invest—for the good of the Kingdom.

Life matters

For many of the clients I advise who have made the leap to Biblically Responsible Investments (BRI), their primary issue is abortion and contraception. Once they are assured that their money will not support either, they don't need to hear anything else. If you share this opinion, you can skip to the next chapter...

But if you want to learn more, there's more.

Every Financial Decision is a Moral Decision

Netzly makes a compelling case: every financial decision is a moral decision. That concept resonated with me and reflects a theme we've returned to throughout this book. As disciples of Christ, we are called to "pray without ceasing" and to "do all for the glory of God" (1 Corinthians 10:31). Every decision has a moral dimension. That includes investing. There are two key elements to a moral decision:

- it must be rightly ordered, and
- it must seek something that is good.

To be rightly ordered, we have to remember that God is the highest good and the source of all good things. We can choose lower goods just for themselves, or we can choose those same goods with gratitude and obedience to God. The first choice is sinful. The second choice is rightly ordered. In both cases, we are choosing a good, but *how* we choose it matters. Fr. Mike Schmitz states this beautifully: "Every sin is an attempt to be happy without God."

So, a rightly ordered investment is one that flows from a heart aligned with God's priorities; gratitude, obedience, and purpose. That doesn't mean every investment has to be labeled

"Christian," but it does mean that the way we invest should be consistent with what we believe God has called us to do. God provides many of us with the ability to save and invest to provide for our families. Retirement accounts, education accounts, and other investment accounts are all good things, but our investments in these accounts should be done in gratitude and in the context of God's plan for us. As we discussed in Chapter 6, *Money Follows Mission.* Our investments should follow that same path so that they are rightly ordered.

Seeking What Is Good

Secondly, we need to choose something that is a good. Growth and profit are good things. Providing for our family's future is a good thing. But what about the companies we're partnering with in our pursuit of those profits? Are they contributing to human flourishing—or diminishing it?

To be a good investment, we should consider what the investment *does*. Proverbs 16:8 reminds us that "better is a little with righteousness than great revenues with injustice." In other words, optimizing for top returns should not be our top priority with our investments.

Ask yourself: Does this company help build a better world? Or is it involved in industries or activities that exploit, degrade, or harm?

Scripture does not shy away from this question. Netzly highlights a striking passage from Deuteronomy 23:18:

> *You shall not bring the fee of a prostitute or the wages of a dog into the house of the Lord your God in payment for any vow, for both of these are an abomination to the Lord your God.*

That's pretty unambiguous—the source of money matters.

If it matters where our money comes from, then it also matters what we're invested in—because investing is simply a way to grow money. But remember: None of it is *our* money. It's all God's. And the portion we're stewarding should be invested in ways that reflect His heart.

Help for Christians Choosing Investments

The good news is that the Biblically Responsible Investment (BRI) industry is growing. And not just in volume, though there has been a significant increase in assets under management by faith-driven investors. It's also growing in quality.

As of the writing of this book, there are a growing number of Christian-owned and run investment firms that have decided to add a Christian Values filter to their investment selection process.

Applying Values to Investing: History

The BRI industry is not the first to apply values to investing. In the last decade some of the major asset managers, including

Blackrock, Vanguard, State Street, and a few others, decided that profit should not be the only criterion for selecting investments. They also believe that every financial decision is a moral decision.

The problem is that their framework for moral decision-making is not a Christian framework, though there is some overlap. Their first framework was called Environmental, Social, Governmental or ESG. Their second framework is called Diversity Equity and Inclusion or DEI. Both of these are humanist attempts to apply moral standards to companies. I applaud their motivation, but as we just discussed, a moral decision needs to be *both* rightly ordered *and* seeking something good.

These two ethical investing frameworks got the second part right (seeking a good), but not the first part (being rightly ordered). Because they are not rightly ordered toward our loving Creator, they also got a few other things wrong. Both frameworks supported and encouraged "women's health" initiatives in corporations, which Christians know are euphemisms for abortion and contraception.

As the decade progressed we also saw them encouraging efforts that undermine God's plan for marriage and families, and more recently promotion of the LGBT+ agenda.

There are plenty of good Christian books about why these movements are disordered, which do a much better job than I can, so I will just say that God created human reason and built us with a desire to seek the good. So these movements all began with good intentions. But because they did not begin by aligning themselves in gratitude and obedience to God's plan for us, they quickly went the way that all purely human endeavors go when divorced from our loving God. When human beings define what is good, we often get it wrong. When we appeal to God, He doesn't get it wrong.

The Christian Response

In the past decade, the BRI industry has seen a tremendous influx, not just of investment dollars from faithful Christians, but a large growth of top quality money managers and analysts; good Christian men and women working at the highest levels of the investing world, who saw what was happening and have found ways to support BRI funds either by changing employers, or more commonly by moonlighting; that is managing sleeves of portfolios for BRI firms in addition to their primary jobs.

Consequently, the quality of investments available to Christian investors has dramatically improved.

Most BRI firms apply a three-part strategy to stewardship:

1. **Negative Screening**
   First, they avoid companies and industries that clearly oppose human flourishing like abortion, contraception, pornography, gambling, tobacco, and related sectors.

2. **Corporate Engagement**
   Second, they actively engage with company leadership. This is about influence—encouraging firms to rethink harmful policies and consider their responsibilities as stewards of their employees, customers, and shareholders. For example, BRI firms have successfully lobbied companies to back away from funding abortion travel benefits or to remove ideological mandates that infringe on religious liberty.

3. **Positive Endorsement**
   Finally, they celebrate and support companies that go beyond neutrality and actively seek to live out Christian values—whether that's through family-friendly policies, charitable giving, or ethical supply chains. Businesses that support crisis pregnancy centers, promote adoption benefits, or encourage employee volunteering with Christian ministries are a few standout examples.

For those of you managing your own portfolios—whether in individual stocks, private businesses, or real estate—you can apply these same filters yourself. It takes time and discernment, but it's doable. And for the many Christians who use managed portfolios, it's a comfort to know there are investment firms that share your biblical worldview.

So... Is Secular Investing a Sin?

No, it's not inherently sinful to invest traditionally. Many Christians own 401(k)s, annuities, or pension funds that offer no biblically screened options. There is no moral guilt in this. Sin involves intent.

If your intent is to provide for your family and your investment choices are limited, God sees your heart. You also are not culpable for decisions made by distant fund managers — especially if those decisions are beyond your control. We are judged by what we know and what we could have done, not by the actions of others outside our knowledge or influence.

That said, we are called to do what we *can* do. And increasingly, what we *can* do is invest more faithfully.

Across denominations, churches are beginning to speak with greater clarity about how faith intersects with finance. Whether Catholic, Evangelical, or Mainline Protestant, the message is consistent:

Our money should reflect our mission. And our investments are part of our witness.

Let's take a moment to explore how these three major streams of Christianity—Catholic, Evangelical, and Mainline Protestant—approach the relationship between faith and finances, particularly as it relates to investing.

Catholic Teaching

The Catholic Church has a rich and well-developed body of teaching on economics and finance, known as **Catholic Social Teaching.** These principles are derived from Scripture and the Church's moral tradition, especially as articulated in papal encyclicals such as *Rerum Novarum*, *Caritas in Veritate*, and *Laudato Si*.

A few key themes stand out:

- **The Universal Destination of Goods**: Private property is affirmed, but it is not absolute. All wealth and resources ultimately belong to God and must be used to benefit the broader human family.
- **The Preferential Option for the Poor**: The poor and vulnerable deserve special concern. Economic decisions—including investing—should consider their impact on human dignity and opportunity.
- **Subsidiarity and Solidarity**: Financial decisions should support local communities (subsidiarity) and promote unity and justice (solidarity).

When it comes to investing, Catholic moral theology does not require divestment from every flawed company, but it encourages active engagement—what the Church calls shareholder advocacy. The U.S. Conference of Catholic Bishops, for example, has published *Socially Responsible Investment Guidelines*, which call for avoiding investments that contradict

Church teaching (such as abortion, pornography, and arms production) and for using shareholder influence to promote ethical behavior in the marketplace.

Catholic teaching sees investing as a moral act that should seek not only profit, but justice, human dignity, and the common good. There is an increasing awareness among Catholic institutions and individuals that investment portfolios should not contradict their moral values.

Evangelical Teaching

Evangelicals tend to emphasize the believer's personal responsibility and the authority of Scripture in all areas of life, including financial stewardship. The biblical call to be a wise steward is deeply rooted in Evangelical culture, particularly through ministries like Crown Financial, Compass Finances, Certified Kingdom Advisors (my professional training background), and the Ron Blue Institute.

Some key principles often emphasized include:

- **God Owns It All**: Everything we have belongs to God. We are stewards, not owners, and that includes our investments.

- **The Heart Behind the Action**: Evangelicals often stress intent and motive. Are we investing to honor God, or to chase security apart from Him?

- **Impact and Witness**: Evangelical leaders have increasingly called for investment strategies that avoid profiting from moral evils like abortion, pornography, and human trafficking. Robert Netzly's work and the rise of **Inspire Investing** and other BRI firms reflect this movement.

While Evangelicals may not have a formal tradition of shareholder engagement like the Catholic Church does, many are now advocating for proactive investing—directing capital toward companies that align with biblical values and away from those that do not. Both Catholic and Evangelical teachings strongly align with BRI.

The Evangelical approach is clear: If you have the ability to invest in ways that align with your faith, you should. More and more options are now available to make that possible.

Mainline Protestant Teaching

Mainline denominations (such as the Presbyterian Church USA, the United Methodist Church, and the Evangelical Lutheran Church in America) have long traditions of connecting faith to social and economic justice. Their investing strategies often fall under the umbrella of **Socially Responsible Investing** (**SRI**).

The emphasis is typically on the following:

- **Justice and Equity**: Investments should support fairness, worker rights, and care for the environment.

- **Creation Care**: Stewardship includes protecting the environment, which leads many denominations to avoid fossil fuels and support sustainable technologies.
- **Corporate Engagement**: Many Mainline denominations actively engage companies through shareholder resolutions, particularly on issues like climate change, racial equity, and labor practices.

Mainline Protestant investment policies sometimes overlap with BRI principles, but there are also key differences. For example, while BRI screens typically exclude companies involved in abortion and contraception, some Mainline groups may not see those issues the same way. Instead, their investment screens often focus more on environmental or labor concerns.

However, the common thread is this: **Investing is not morally neutral**. Whether for a denomination, a foundation, or an individual, Mainline traditions assert that Christians are responsible for the effects of how and where they invest.

Common Ground and the Way Forward

While the starting points and emphases may differ, all three traditions agree on this core idea:

Christians should invest in a way that reflects the heart of God.

Whether it's called Biblically Responsible Investing, Faith- Based Investing, or Socially Responsible Investing, the goal is the same: to align your capital with your convictions.

That doesn't necessarily mean you must sell everything and start over. But it does mean asking new questions:

- What does this company stand for?
- Is this investment consistent with what I believe about God and human dignity?
- Am I stewarding His resources with both wisdom and faith?

Faithful investing is not about legalism or perfection. It's about discipleship. It's about aligning our portfolios with our prayers. And it's about remembering that our investments are not just financial tools—but also spiritual ones—just like everything else we steward.

CHAPTER 8

Structured Philanthropy: Tools and Reasons

As for the rich in this world, charge them not to set their hopes on uncertain riches, but on GOD who richly furnishes us with everything to enjoy. Command them to do good, to be rich in good deeds, and to be generous and willing to share.
— 1 Timothy 6:17–18

This chapter goes a bit deeper into structured giving and philanthropy. If you're not yet ready to go beyond tithing and almsgiving, feel free to skip it. I'm including it because some of you *are* ready—and these are the kinds of questions Kingdom Advisors get regularly.

What Comes After Tithing and Almsgiving?

When we tithe, we unite our hearts with God's generous and loving nature by returning our first fruits to Him through His Church. When we give alms, we live out our prayer, becoming the hands and feet of the Holy Spirit. We respond to the call of Matthew 25:40: "Whatever you did for one of the least of these brothers and sisters of mine, you did for me." We give spontaneously from our wants to the needs of others, prompted by the Spirit.

But sometimes, God calls us to more.

Some of us have been abundantly blessed with resources far beyond our personal needs. With that abundance comes a responsibility to steward those resources well and advance the Kingdom in broader ways.

> *To whom much is given, much is required.*
>
> —Luke 12:48.

Wealth can be heady. Our culture admires it—sometimes worships it. But it can corrupt if it isn't rightly ordered. The Bible is full of warnings about the misuse of material wealth.

To a faithful steward, though, wealth becomes a weighty calling—a tool for larger Kingdom impact. This kind of stewardship demands wisdom, broader awareness, and above all, prayer.

> *A man's heart plans his way, but the Lord directs his steps.*
>
> — Proverbs 16:9

Before we act with these extra resources we are stewards of, we should research our community's or the world's needs, understand the tools available to help address those needs, and then take our plans to God in prayer.

Trust the Holy Spirit

God often changes our plans in prayer, which can be frustrating after the work we put into planning things. But God sees all, so He sees what we cannot. He sees all of time at the same time, so He sees future consequences of current actions that we simply do not have the perspective or wisdom to see or anticipate.

A significant mystery of this level of generosity is that God requires us to lean in and lead, but in order to be rightly ordered work, in service of His Kingdom, using His resources, we have to follow His Will, not ours. I was on a school board several years ago, and I had some ideas to address the issues the board was wrestling with. I had seen these ideas work in other schools in similar situations, and I was willing to financially support the implementation of the ideas.

I presented my ideas to the board and was soundly rejected. In prayer, I asked God why he let this fail, and got back in prayer "*did I ask you to fix those problems?*" He let me know that those problems were someone else's challenge.

I should have checked with God first. This episode helped me to begin trusting the Holy Spirit's power and dominion over our church and school more, and recognize that I am a pawn in a multi-dimensional game of chess. I need to serve where I am directed. And I need to ask and listen to God before acting, including Him in my decisions big and small.

God's plan for the school–and for my life–is a mystery to me. I love mysteries like this. I believe that these mysteries keep us on our toes and draw us into God's incredible majesty, building into us humility and a healthy fear and love of God as we recognize just how little God needs us and at the same time how much He desires us, with His infinite love (and patience) to join Him in the work of serving His people and having dominion over His world!

Called to More

Entering into God's generosity does not need to mean that we give away all of the money that we don't need. Some of us ARE called to lives of radical poverty, or to serve the poor directly. If you are called that way, REJOICE! You are being called to join a long history of disciples and saints who, unlike the young man with many possessions who walked away saddened, have detached from their possessions and found their joy in trusting God's providence! That is true wealth, stored up in Heaven.

But many of us *have been* entrusted with more wealth and are called in other ways to serve the Kingdom. That's the point of this book, to explore the responsibilities of wealth.

The Role of Capitalism

The surest way to lift someone out of poverty is to give them meaningful employment—work that allows them to provide for themselves and their families. Entrepreneurs, business owners, and business leaders serve the Kingdom daily in this vital way—most of them don't even realize it!

Businesses are engines of wealth creation. Bottom-line profits can be used in three essential ways:

1. **Capital Reinvestment**:
   Profits can be reinvested back into the business to increase revenue or decrease expenses.

   The Kingdom impact is found in serving more people with your goods or services. God may also call you to serve His Kingdom by expanding your business and employing more people. This requires prudence, careful planning—and, always, prayer.

2. **Investment in Other Enterprises**:
   Profits can also be deployed by investing in other businesses, achieving similar results indirectly. Care should be taken to invest in ways that support the Kingdom. Consider reviewing where your capital is deployed, applying the BRI principles we discussed last chapter to your analysis, and praying over those investments. (We covered this more fully in the previous chapter.)

   Most of the "wealth" that wealthy stewards have is actually tied up in one of these two categories — either reinvested or invested elsewhere. The wealth isn't just sitting idle; it's out doing more work for the Kingdom! Perhaps it could be managed more intentionally and prayerfully, but it's not being buried in the ground like the unfaithful servant in Jesus' parable.

3. **Philanthropy:**
   The third use of profits involves giving them away to serve others—and that is what the rest of this chapter will explore.

From Almsgiving to Philanthropy

Alms usually respond to immediate needs — feeding the hungry, helping a neighbor after a fire, or buying someone warm clothes. These are beautiful, Spirit-led responses.

Philanthropy often has a longer arc. Over time, it builds capacity—organizations, missions, schools, medical outreaches—that serve *many* of God's children. It's no less spiritual, just different in scale and structure.

When giving money away, it is wise to ask a few key questions:

1. What is good for the recipient?
2. What is the Kingdom impact of the gift?
3. What is the most efficient and effective way to give?

When we give alms, we often see the immediate need we are meeting. We feed the hungry, clothe the naked, shelter the homeless—responding to needs the Holy Spirit has drawn to our attention. Almsgiving can range from small acts, like offering a granola bar to a homeless person, to major sacrifices, like using a vacation fund to help a neighbor whose house has burned down.

Philanthropy, or structured giving, usually targets longer-term or larger-scale Kingdom projects. Where almsgiving often helps one of God's children immediately, philanthropy builds or supports organizations designed to help many of God's children over time.

There is significant overlap between the two, and you could argue that philanthropy is simply another form of almsgiving, that they are different mainly in scope. Both are Spirit-led responses to the needs around us. That's a worthy discussion! But for the purposes of this book, I'm separating them to explore the practical tools available to stewards who are called to give and serve through the wealth they have been entrusted with.

What's Good for the Recipient?

A nonprofit I used to work with shared this story, and I think it's a perfect illustration:

Imagine standing next to a river. Suddenly, you see someone floating downstream, struggling. You jump in and pull them to safety. Before you can catch your breath, you see another person coming. And another. Pretty soon, you and your friends are working together, pulling person after person from the river. It's hard, holy work.

Then somebody asks: *Why are people falling into the river in the first place?*

Should we just keep pulling them out—or should someone go upstream and see if there's a way to stop it from happening?

Both are good and necessary. Rescuing people matters deeply. But some of us are also called to go upstream to tackle the root causes, to build something that changes the future.

As stewards, part of our role is prayerfully asking: *Where is God calling me to help?* Downstream, upstream, or maybe a little of both?

Both are Kingdom work.

Impact Efficiency and Tax Efficiency

Effective stewards also consider two practical aspects of their giving: **impact efficiency** and **tax efficiency**.

Impact Efficiency

Impact efficiency means considering how the size and timing of a gift can maximize its effect.

For example:

- A gift given during a fundraising campaign could be used as a matching challenge, encouraging others to give more.
- A well-timed gift could help an organization secure a major grant.

- Regular gifts could ease the burden of recurring costs like payroll, mission trip expenses, or operational needs.

Sometimes making the greatest impact simply means adjusting the timing by a few weeks. Other times, it may require longer-term planning, especially for major projects like building a church or launching a new ministry.

Tax Efficiency

Now let's talk about another important piece of the puzzle: tax efficiency.

Good stewards know that if they plan their giving wisely, they might be able to pay less in taxes, which means more resources can go to the Kingdom causes God has placed on their hearts.

Philanthropy often involves simply writing checks, and that's fine. But if you're willing to plan a little, you can often do even better. Giving cash is easy—you just write a check. However, giving appreciated assets, like stocks or mutual funds, is often far more tax-efficient.

Here's how it works:
Instead of selling a highly appreciated investment (and paying taxes on the gain), you can transfer shares directly to a charity or church.

You receive a tax deduction for the full fair market value of the gift, and the charity can sell the investments *tax-free* to fund their mission.

If you sell the investment first you'll have to pay capital gains taxes, which means a smaller donation and a smaller impact.

But if you give the asset directly?

Everyone wins.

There's another powerful tool available, too, especially for those over 70½ years old:

If you have money in a Traditional IRA (or old workplace retirement plans like 401(k)s, 403(b)s, or 457 plans), you can make a Qualified Charitable Distribution (QCD) directly to a church or charity. The gift counts toward your Required Minimum Distribution (RMD) but doesn't get counted as taxable income. It's currently the *only way* to get money out of these tax-sheltered retirement accounts without paying taxes on the withdrawal!

For larger or more complex gifts such as real estate, private business interests, or other illiquid assets, there are even more strategies.

These gifts usually require careful planning and might involve using tools like *charitable remainder trusts, charitable lead trusts, donor-advised funds*, or *private foundations*. They take a little more time and teamwork (you'll definitely want your financial advisor, attorney, and tax advisor all involved together), but they can often save you significant taxes— allowing you to give even more generously in the future.

Important disclaimer:

Tax laws vary by country, and even in the United States, they change often. Always consult with your financial, tax, and legal advisors before making decisions. Think of them as your stewardship team helping you be as faithful and effective as possible.

Structured Giving Tools for Stewards

When stewards feel called to give in bigger or more sustained ways, it's helpful to know about the different tools available. These aren't just financial strategies—they are ways to *steward the resources God has entrusted to us* with wisdom, creativity, and impact.

Here are a few of the most common tools available in the United States at the time of this writing:

1. **Donor-Advised Funds (DAFs)**
   A Donor-Advised Fund is a simple, flexible way to organize your giving.

   Here's how it works:

   - You make a charitable contribution to a DAF account, where it can be invested and grow tax-free.

- You receive an immediate tax deduction for the contribution.
- Later, you recommend grants to charities from the DAF—at your own pace.

Think of it like having your own mini charitable foundation but without all the paperwork and administrative hassle.

DAFs can be a great fit in the following scenarios if:

- You want to bunch several years' worth of giving into one tax year.
- You want time to prayerfully discern where your gifts should go.
- You want your giving to continue even after you're gone, with your children or grandchildren making future grant recommendations.

2. **Charitable Trusts**

   Charitable trusts are a little more complex, but offer some unique benefits.

   There are two main types:

   - **Charitable Remainder Trusts (CRTs)**: You (or someone you name) receive income from the trust for a period of time. After that, the remainder goes to a charity you choose.

- **Charitable Lead Trusts (CLTs)**: The charity gets income first for a set period, and then the remainder goes to your heirs or other beneficiaries.

These structures can be powerful tools for reducing estate taxes, providing for family members, and making a significant Kingdom impact.

They do require legal setup and ongoing management, so they're usually best suited for larger gifts or more complex financial situations.

3. **Private Foundations**
Private foundations are the most involved option. They require forming a legal entity, complying with specific rules, and filing annual tax returns.

However, they offer maximum control:

- You can hire staff, including family members.
- You can create your own grant-making programs.
- You can set the mission and priorities for generations to come.

Private foundations are usually best for stewards who

- Want to involve their family across multiple generations.
- Plan to give away substantial assets.
- Are willing to take on administrative responsibilities (or hire professionals to help).

Important Reminder:
Each tools has legal, tax, and financial implications. Choosing the right structure (or combination) depends on your specific calling, your financial situation, and the needs you feel led to meet. Please work with your financial advisor, attorney, and tax professional to design a plan that fits your stewardship journey.

Why Structured Philanthropy Matters

At first glance, structured giving might seem complicated, full of legal terms, tax considerations, and paperwork. It's easy to wonder: *Why not just write a check when I feel led? Isn't that simpler and more Spirit-led?*

Sometimes, yes! Immediate, spontaneous generosity is a beautiful act of obedience.

But in many cases, structuring your giving wisely can actually multiply your impact, extend your reach, and strengthen the ministries or missions God has called you to support.

Structured philanthropy matters because

- **It can make your gifts go farther.**
  Careful planning can help ministries receive larger, more consistent support—and sometimes even unlock matching grants or other outside funding.

- **It can make your giving more sustainable.**
  Instead of a one-time gift, structured strategies can fund Kingdom work for years, or even generations.

- **It can free you to give more.**
  By being mindful of taxes and timing, you may find you're able to give more than you ever thought possible, simply by being wise with what God has entrusted to you.

In the end, structured philanthropy is simply a way to align good intentions with good stewardship, putting our hands and feet in the Spirit's service with as much care and prayer as any other part of the Christian life.

Let's explore some of the main reasons stewards choose to give this way—and how you can think about it in your own journey.

Reasons Stewards Choose Structured Giving

1. **To Amplify Impact**
   When you structure your giving—through things like matching gifts, timed donations, or strategic grants—you can actually encourage others to give alongside you. One generous act can become many. A single gift might inspire an entire community, or help an organization meet a critical milestone faster. Structured giving isn't just about writing a bigger check; it's about multiplying the effect of every dollar for the Kingdom.

2. **To Support Ministry Stability**
   Many ministries struggle not because they lack vision or passion, but because they face unpredictable funding. Structured gifts—like endowments, multi - year commitments, or well-timed grants—can help ministries plan ahead, hire well, and stay focused on their mission instead of constantly scrambling for survival. Your planning today can give them the stability to dream bigger tomorrow.

3. **To Build a Legacy of Faithfulness**
   Some giving opportunities are designed to outlast us. Through trusts, foundations, or donor-advised funds, stewards can create structures that **continue to** support Kingdom work even after we've gone home to be with the Lord. It's a beautiful way to make your final testimony one of generosity, vision, and enduring faith.

4. **To Increase Stewardship Capacity**
   Sometimes, structured giving allows you to give more without sacrificing other stewardship responsibilities. For example, using appreciated assets (like stocks or real estate) instead of cash can allow you to avoid taxes, freeing up more resources for giving. Or spreading a large commitment over several years can allow you to give more overall, while still meeting family needs and obligations. It's not about being clever with money— it's about being faithful with the whole picture God has given you.

5. **To Follow the Spirit with Wisdom and Care**
   Not every gift needs a complex structure. Sometimes the Holy Spirit calls for immediate, generous action—and we obey. Other times, the Spirit invites us to think, pray, plan, and partner with others to accomplish something bigger than we could do alone. Structured philanthropy simply gives you tools to respond wisely when God calls you to bigger things.

CHAPTER 9

Stewardship of a Business

Be sure you know the condition of your flocks, give careful attention to your herds; for riches do not endure forever, and a crown is not secure for all generations.

—Proverbs 27:23 – 24

Business owners have added dimensions of stewardship concerns. If you own a business with employees, you know this already. You have close relationships with some of your clients and feel a responsibility to them. Your employees may feel like your children, and you may feel keenly the responsibility to provide a good life for their families as well as your own.

What you may not know is that somewhere around 50% of business exits are involuntary due to the "Five Ds"— Death, Disability, Divorce, Distress, or Disagreement. Of the businesses that attempt an intentional transition, only about 20% to 30% actually succeed in selling or transitioning ownership as planned. These are the current realities according to the Exit Planning Institute (EPI). While there may be some variation internationally, these challenges appear fairly universal.

Some amount of creative destruction is part of God's design. We see it in nature, the cycle of birth, life, decline, and death. Some businesses solve problems that are no longer problems, like the overused "buggy whip" example from the early 1900s when the automobile replaced the horse and buggy. More recent examples include the disappearance of dry cleaners as clothing trends move toward casual wear, the obsolescence of CD players and MP3 players with the rise of streaming music, and the extinction of paper road maps and atlases with GPS apps on our phones.

However, many businesses could survive and continue serving clients and providing for employees' families with the application of stewardship principles.

One of the biggest challenges facing business owners who sell their businesses is regret. According to EPI research, over 75% of owners profoundly regret selling their business within a year after the transition. Why? For many owners, the business was a primary source of identity and purpose. Many owners describe their business as their "child."

If we have made the transition to discipleship in other areas of life—entrusting wealth, homes, our marriages, and our children to Christ—then doing the same with our businesses should be a natural next step. Yet these statistics and the experience of business exit coaches suggest otherwise.

I am not going to go into great detail about business exit planning; there are entire books on that topic already. I will, however, give you a few ideas to help you transition to a stewardship relationship with your business.

Prayer, of course, must be at the heart of this planning. The Holy Spirit may have a plan for your business that you have not considered—or would not choose for yourself. You won't know until you ask.

Begin with the End in Mind

Start as early as possible by thinking of your business as something transferrable. A transferrable business is one that can largely run itself day-to-day, requiring only vision, purpose, and capital decisions from the owner. Think of the vineyard owner in Jesus' parables, who sent his servants to manage the vineyard without his constant presence.

Building transferability requires intentionality. Businesses that rely heavily on the owner's personal skills and relationships are usually not transferrable. So, creating systems for hiring, training, and client relationship management is good stewardship.

The founder or owner must gradually separate from the daily operations. We often hear that business owners should work on the business as well as in the business. Working toward transferability forces you to follow through—until the business barely needs you to run smoothly.

Identify Possible Next Stewards and Prepare Them.

The next steward could be:

- A family member
- A key employee
- A group of employees
- A competitor
- An outside private equity firm
- A complete stranger

If your likely successor is a family member like a child, niece, or nephew, have you positioned them to learn the necessary skills? Some stewards raise their children in the business, teaching them from the bottom up. Others require their children to work elsewhere first, to gain broader experience before returning. There's no "right" method, but intentional preparation is crucial.

And remember: Their good comes first, followed by the good of the business. God's plan for them may be different from yours. It may involve leading another business, starting a nonprofit, serving in missions, becoming a pastor or priest, or something else entirely.

Timing is Critical.

Be ready to hand over the business *when the next steward is ready*—not when you're finally ready to let go. I have seen heartbreaking situations where owners clung too long, only to find that their children moved on, and the once-valuable business was no longer transferable. Turning 80 and facing a business closure alone is a very sad reality for many.

Businesses are most transferable at their peak value, which often coincides with the owner's peak vitality. In most cases, transitions should happen when owners are in their 50s or early 60s. Waiting longer often leads to slower growth, business decline, loss of key people (kids or key employees who decided not to stick around any longer waiting, and got on with their lives), and diminished market value.

It's a tragedy when businesses that once supported dozens of families, sponsored community sports teams, and contributed generously to local causes, fade away simply because of delayed stewardship decisions.

Stewardship thinking can help owners avoid this sad outcome.

> Train the young in the way they should go; even when old, they will not swerve from it.
>
> — Proverbs 22:6

A faithful steward prepares the next steward, considering *their* timing, family situation, and future.

Practical Transition Structures

There are several ways to transition businesses:

Transition to Children

Transitions to children are often simpler in structure but require careful preparation and a lot of grace, especially when fairness among siblings must be considered. Preparing a child for ownership can take years, but the actual transfer may be relatively simple.

Transition to a Key Employee

Transitions to employees often require more financial planning. Unlike family members, employees typically cannot buy a business outright without outside funding.

One structure I have seen work is the *three-stage structured sale*:

- **Stage 1:**
  The owner "sells" a 49% stake at a 50% discount, self-financing the deal. Dividends from the business pay down the "loan" on paper, usually over 2–3 years.

- **Stage 2:**
  Once the first loan is repaid, the employee (now 49% owner) secures a bank loan to buy the remaining 51%, ideally at an increased valuation if the business has grown under their younger, enthusiastic leadership.

- **Stage 3:**
  The owner signs a consulting contract, to assist for 1–2 years after the sale. The value of this contract can mirror the original 25% discount from Stage 1.

This approach can keep businesses alive in communities, preserve wealth, protect jobs, and create bright futures for the next generation of owners.

Transition to Multiple Employees

Businesses with 50+ employees often sell to groups of employees through direct sales or employee stock ownership plans (ESOPs). ESOPs can provide significant tax advantages and allow broader employee participation. Specialized advisors should guide these more complex transitions. Transition tools also differ in different countries, and even year-to-year as tax and corporate laws change. It can be wise to use advisors for these transfers.

Two Vital Areas for Prayer and Planning

1. **The Process of Transition:**
   Always remember that the business is God's. You have been a faithful steward. Now, it is someone else's turn. Pray that your plans will prioritize the good of employees, clients, the community, and the next steward.

2. **Your Next Purpose:**
   Most business sellers who experience regret after a transition had no clear sense of what came next. Those who thrive after selling their business move with purpose toward the next calling God has for them.

   This calling could involve:

   - More time with grandchildren
   - Starting a new business or nonprofit
   - Serving on boards
   - Mentoring entrepreneurs
   - Teaching
   - Volunteering
   - Traveling and exploring God's creation
   - Playing endless rounds of golf

The key is to prayerfully craft a written plan for your next phase of life, submit it to God, and allow Him to order your steps.

PART IV

Stewardship of Legacy

CHAPTER 10

Memento Mori – Preparing for What Comes Next

All go to one place; all are from the dust,
and all turn to dust again.
— Ecclesiastes 3:20

Memento mori—Latin for "Remember your death"—has echoed through history for centuries. In ancient Rome, it was custom for a slave to whisper this phrase into the ear of a victorious general, a reminder that even in triumph, mortality was inescapable. As Christianity spread, the church adopted this tradition as a tool for spiritual reflection. The phrase found its way onto signet rings, into Shakespearean plays, and deeply into Western tradition.

The Bible reinforces this theme:

> *Remember you are dust, and to dust you shall return*
> — Genesis 3:19

For Christians, remembering our mortality isn't meant to inspire fear, it is meant to ground us. It is a sober reminder that everything we are and everything we steward belongs to God.

The Steward's Question: What Comes After Death?

As stewards of God's gifts, we must ask not just, "*Who inherits my assets?*" but rather, "*Who will be the next steward of what God has entrusted to me?*"

Inheritance implies ownership. Stewardship, however, acknowledges that we are managing what ultimately belongs to the Lord. This shift in perspective radically changes how we think about estate planning. It's not merely about transferring wealth; it's about transferring responsibility, discipleship, and trust.

Stewardship vs. Ownership: A Different Lens

Let's challenge a deeply ingrained idea: *Who loves your children more—you or God?*

While most of us would quickly answer, "God," internalizing that truth can be harder. Our culture emphasizes ownership—even of our children's futures. Yet stewardship invites us to trust that God has a far greater and better plan for their lives than we ever could.

This truth changes how we view estate planning. Traditional estate planning often centers on preserving and passing on wealth. Wealth becomes the end goal. Without realizing it, we may begin serving wealth rather than allowing wealth to serve God's purposes. That is the danger of an ownership mentality: we become servants of our possessions.

Through the lens of stewardship, we instead ask:

What is God's plan for this wealth, and when does He want it passed to the next steward?

What Is the Role of the Next Steward?

Stewardship-centered estate planning asks:

- What do the next stewards need?
- What is God's plan for them?
- When do they need resources?
- What role is this wealth intended to play in their lives?

Traditional estate planning usually transfers assets at death, largely for tax reasons. But that often ignores the question of timing—God's timing. Sometimes, earlier transfer might be more fruitful for the Kingdom, even if it is less efficient financially.

Here is Where Tax Consequences Matter.

Under current U.S. tax law (and this changes often, so be sure to understand the laws when you are planning), most assets receive a "step-up" in cost basis at death. This means that if your children sell the inherited stock or real estate, they usually won't owe taxes on the accumulated gains.

If you sell the assets during your lifetime to give them cash, *you* will pay the taxes on the gains. If you gift the assets outright during your lifetime, *they* receive your original cost basis — and may owe substantial taxes when they eventually sell.

In simple terms:

- Hold an asset until death → heirs inherit with no (or reduced) taxes.
- Gift an asset during life → heirs inherit your original cost basis and may owe taxes.

Thus, if the goal is to maximize the amount passed on to the next stewards, we are often encouraged to "hold on" to assets until death.

But stewardship invites a harder, more prayerful question:

What does God want to be passed to the next steward, and when?

Stewards prioritize the good of the Kingdom over the good of the asset. We look outward: at our children's lives, our churches, our communities, our businesses, and our employees — *before* looking inward at what benefits the assets themselves.

And we pray.

We pray that God will align our priorities with His. If God calls us to act in ways that are not tax-efficient but are timely and Kingdom-focused, we must be willing to follow His will.

That said, there are many ways to be both faithful and prudent. As we discussed in the previous chapter, strategies like pairing gifts to heirs with charitable donations can offset tax impacts. Good advisors can help you design plans that are both wise and generous.

We are not called to be reckless. We are called to be careful, prayerful, and strategic stewards of our Master's wealth.

Stewardship Estate Planning Considerations

Stewardship-based estate planning begins with a strong financial plan. As discussed earlier, this includes asking, *"How much is enough?"* for our own lives—identifying our finish lines. When we know how much is enough for our needs, we can see more clearly what assets we are carrying on behalf of others.

Understanding our children's "finish lines" can be just as important.

Some children choose lives of service—pastors, missionaries, teachers, parents raising large families—where additional financial support may be needed. Other children may be financially independent, requiring little or no inheritance.

This information, taken to prayer, gives us the wisdom to craft a plan that matches God's will.

Attorneys, by necessity, often default to simple, tax-efficient estate plans because they cannot know the nuances of your family's needs and calling. It is not unreasonable; they must work with the information they have.

But when you, as a steward, come prepared with deeper spiritual and practical insights, it becomes possible to craft an estate plan that is more personal, more detailed, and more faithful.

In the next chapter, we will discuss how to work with attorneys and advisors to create a plan that reflects this stewardship mindset.

Are the Next Stewards Prepared?

Stewards are God's hands and feet in the world. Our greatest impact may not come through the wealth we manage, but through the stewards we raise up after us.

Scripture is clear about this responsibility:

And you shall teach them diligently to your children, and shall talk of them when you sit in your house, when you walk by the way, when you lie down, and when you rise up.
— Deuteronomy 6:7

Train up a child in the way he should go; even when he is old he will not depart from it.
— Proverbs 22:6

Our stewardship ripples across generations. The poor we serve, the disciples we help, the children we teach—all of these create a ripple effect of Kingdom work that extends far beyond our lifetimes.

If your children are young, teaching them about stewardship can be a joyful, daily part of life.

Teach them to tithe, to budget, to save, and to invest according to God's plan. Make stewardship a family conversation. There are excellent resources for families who want to raise generous, faithful children.

But if you came to deep discipleship later in life, as I did, you may find it harder to prepare adult children who grew up with a different worldview. Patience will be necessary. Example will be necessary. It may take years before they fully understand your shift from ownership to stewardship.

Each child is on their own journey. Some will embrace stewardship quickly. Some will struggle. Some may wander for a time.

Two forces are at work: their free will, and the Holy Spirit.

Trust the Holy Spirit.

The Challenge of Adult Children: A Stewardship Journey

When children seem to be going astray, parents often wrestle with painful decisions about stewardship.

Jesus said:

> *Which of you, if your son asks for bread, will give him a stone? Or if he asks for a fish, will give him a snake?*
> — Matthew 7:9

Some parents, facing children who are trapped in destructive lifestyles—addiction, chronic irresponsibility— choose to exclude them from their estates for the child's protection. In cases like serious drug addiction, money could literally be fatal. Prayerful discernment is crucial here.

But there is another lens to consider—the story of the prodigal son.

The father, knowing his son was immature and reckless, gave him a full inheritance anyway. The son squandered it all. Yet in the end, the story is not one of loss—it is one of redemption.

The son returned, broken but repentant. The money was lost, but the soul was saved.

Everything belongs to the Father in Heaven.

If God uses what we consider "wasted" wealth to bring a wandering child home, then was it truly wasted? Or was it used precisely according to God's perfect, mysterious purposes?

If you were hoping for a simple formula to guide your estate planning when your family is less than perfect, here it is:

Pray and trust the Holy Spirit.

Then take what you hear in prayer to your financial planner and attorney.

Memento mori calls us to live—and to plan—with eternity in view. As stewards, we are not merely passing on assets; we are passing on a testimony of trust in God's provision and purposes. In the next chapter, we will turn to the practical steps of working with advisors and crafting estate plans that do more than just transfer wealth and avoid taxes. They will tell a story, a story of faith, stewardship, and love for the One who owns it all.

CHAPTER 11

Don't Go It Alone — Why Godly Counsel is the Key to Lifelong Stewardship

---

Plans are established by counsel; by wise guidance wage war.
— Proverbs 20:18

Over the past chapters, we've walked through a radical shift in perspective—away from the ownership model the which the world promotes and toward a biblical vision of stewardship, where everything belongs to God and we are His trusted managers.

But here's the truth: even the clearest convictions can drift if they're not anchored in wise community. And even the best intentions can falter without godly guidance.

Counsel matters—not as a footnote to your stewardship but as a foundation for living it out over a lifetime.

The Crossroads of Success

If God has entrusted you with wealth, you will face moments of decision that test your convictions:

- A lucrative business sale that could change your family's trajectory.
- A windfall inheritance that comes with complexity.
- A season of plenty that stirs questions of purpose. The world says: "You've earned it. You're in control."

But Scripture says: "You're a steward. Be faithful."

> *Without counsel plans fail,*
> *but with many advisers they succeed.*
> — Proverbs 15:22

The Wrong Kind of Counsel Can Still Sound Smart

Many believers unknowingly surround themselves with advisors who, though skilled and even Christian by profession, still operate from an ownership worldview. I know because this was me. I brought my faith to the office and treated everyone with Christian love and respect. I made sure that I served anyone who walked through my door, not just the ones with large accounts. I was a financial advisor who was Christian. But I was not a Christian Financial Advisor.

I didn't know what I didn't know. I had a client who utterly confused me because he led me through the processes I have discussed in this book, including the setting of finish lines, and then started talking about giving away everything else. I helped him to the best of my ability to think through ways to give away wealth. But I was confused. This did not make sense given my very high-quality financial education and decade and a half of experience.

Then I found CKA training (Certified Kingdom Advisor) and as I studied how to apply Biblical wisdom to my job, the veil was lifted, and my ownership worldview was shattered.

I couldn't see the world the same way ever again. It really is a different way to be an advisor. I was a good mammon advisor for most of my career, but now I had to rethink everything.

What's the difference? There are many good Christians who are advisors, attorneys and CPAs. They'll help you build, protect, and grow your wealth—but rarely challenge you to surrender it to the Master.

There's a subtle danger in that.

You might still tithe, donate generously, and use Christian language—yet still make decisions based on fear, control, or legacy-building that subtly centers your goals instead of the Master's.

God isn't asking for religious financial planning. He's asking for relational surrender—where your wealth follows your walk.

Christ calls us to follow God, not mammon. That's hard. That's as hard as being a camel, trying to get through the eye of a needle. It's harder if your wise counsel is still rooted in the worldview of mammon.

The Steward's Inner Circle

If you want to keep walking this narrow road of faithful stewardship, you need people around you who will:

- Remind you of what's truly yours — and what's not.
- Help you navigate complexity with eternal clarity.
- Ask hard questions when the culture whispers, "You deserve more."

> *Iron sharpens iron, and one man sharpens another.*
> — Proverbs 27:17

Godly counsel doesn't just protect your net worth. It strengthens your soul.

Create Your Advisors

So what can you do to surround yourself with good counselors? Generally speaking there are two options. You can *create* them or you can *find* them.

You hopefully have advisors around you that you like and trust. Most likely they are good Christians who are walking in discipleship in other parts of their lives. But, they don't know what they don't know, like I didn't before I received training that opened my eyes.

You have an opportunity to guide them! Explain your desire to live as a steward. Share this book with them. Offer to explore this world of stewardship with them, letting them "experiment" with you. Help them find Kingdom-focused resources and education for them, whether they are financial advisors, attorneys, or accountants. You could open up for them a world of discipleship that they didn't know existed and through your witness, impact many more lives.

or Find Your Advisors

Leading your advisor may not be possible, either because you can't find a good advisor who values discipleship, or because they are unwilling to follow you on this journey. It's understandable. If they are a good advisor, they may be so busy and successful doing business the world's way that the thought of risking all of that success is frightening. Their success is feeding their family, and they are doing good works with it. Just before telling us the camel parable, Christ called a good, faithful young man to leave his possessions and follow Him; "*At that saying his countenance fell and he went away sorrowful; for he had great possessions.*" You can be sad for them, but you can't force them to follow you.

So, if you can't create Christian advisors, you may need to find them. Currently the Certified Kingdom Advisor program trains financial advisors, attorneys and CPAs and is the leader in the United States for this education. The industry of Christian advisors is growing rapidly though, so by the time you read this book there may be more options available.

If you can't find a trained advisor locally, don't be afraid to expand your search. Good advisors can serve clients nationally, and technology makes those relationships possible.

A Final Word: Don't Walk Alone

Jesus said it would be hard for the rich to enter the Kingdom —not because wealth is evil, but because it deceives us into thinking we're self-sufficient. This book has been about waking up from that illusion, about re-centering your wealth—and your heart—on Christ.

The truth is that the wealthy *cannot* enter heaven by their own efforts. None of us can. All of us must detach from the things of this world and kneel in humble submission to the Master who will draw us up into heaven. Wealth makes it more difficult to walk the narrow road.

But no one walks the narrow road alone.

So as you leave these pages and enter real-life stewardship, don't go it alone.

Seek out faithful voices. Submit your plans to prayer. Surround yourself with counsel that loves Jesus more than spreadsheets.

And when you're tempted to take back control, remember who the real Owner is—and how much love He is showing you through what has been entrusted to you.

You've been given much. Now walk in wisdom.

Not just for your own sake, but for the glory of God, the good of others, and the joy of a life well-stewarded.

> *It is required of stewards that they be found faithful.*
> — 1 Corinthians 4:2

CONCLUSION

Well Done, Good and Faithful Steward

At the end of a faithful steward's life, the true reward is not measured in bank balances, influence, or even good works. It is found in the words of the Master:

Well done, good and faithful servant. Enter into the joy of your Lord.

A life of stewardship is a life of joyful obedience. It is not burdened by guilt, nor driven by fear, but filled with trust. It begins with small steps—setting priorities, examining our budgets, investing wisely, giving generously and preparing those who come after us—and it builds into a legacy that honors the Giver above all gifts.

You were made for a purpose. Your resources were entrusted to you for a purpose. None of it is random, and none of it is yours to cling to forever. God calls you to be a manager, not an owner, and He equips you with every grace you need to live out that calling.

As you walk forward from here, know that stewardship is not about perfection. It is about faithfulness. It is about learning, failing, trying again, and keeping your eyes on Christ, who promises to complete the good work He has begun in you.

May your life be a living testimony that money is not your master, Christ is.

May your wealth—whether little or great—point beyond itself to the One who gave everything for you.

And may you, on that final day, hear those precious words:

Well done, good and faithful servant.

✦ Continue the Journey ✦

This book is just the beginning. If you'd like to go deeper into the daily practice of stewardship - I invite you to visit the Eye of the Needle blog.

Simply scan the QR code or visit eyeoftheneedlebook.org to explore more. Let's keep growing together as faithful stewards.

The Eye of the Needle Prayer

God, help me to be a good camel.

To recognize that everything I carry is Yours. Some is Your gift to me from Your generous and loving heart. Some I carry for others. Help me to share with others, recognizing that it is not my love and generosity at work but that it is Your love and generosity flowing through me.

And when it is time to pass through the narrow gate, help me to joyfully pass Your gifts to the next steward, and as an obedient camel, help me to kneel humbly before You that You may carry me into Your holy city.

Amen.

ABOUT THE AUTHOR

Dan Hamlet is a Kingdom Financial Advisor, Army Reserve Lieutenant Colonel, Husband and father of 7 children, and founder and CEO of of 360 Integrated Financial, a financial advising firm specializing in helping people and business owners plan as Stewards and invest in biblically responsible ways.

He and Jennifer are raising their children in lovely rural southern Minnesota, where they stay deeply involved with church life, children's sports, pro-life ministries and feeding anyone who will sit for a moment.

Made in the USA
Monee, IL
08 August 2025

2aaf69d1-b743-44c3-976d-845b114ba507R01